OCEANS ALIVE

Frogfish

by Colleen Sexton

BELLWETHER MEDIA · MINNEAPOLIS, MN

Note to Librarians, Teachers, and Parents:

Blastoff! Readers are carefully developed by literacy experts and combine standards-based content with developmentally appropriate text.

Level 1 provides the most support through repetition of high-frequency words, light text, predictable sentence patterns, and strong visual support.

Level 2 offers early readers a bit more challenge through varied simple sentences, increased text load, and less repetition of high-frequency words.

Level 3 advances early-fluent readers toward fluency through increased text and concept load, less reliance on visuals, longer sentences, and more literary language.

Level 4 builds reading stamina by providing more text per page, increased use of punctuation, greater variation in sentence patterns, and increasingly challenging vocabulary.

Level 5 encourages children to move from "learning to read" to "reading to learn" by providing even more text, varied writing styles, and less familiar topics.

Whichever book is right for your reader, Blastoff! Readers are the perfect books to build confidence and encourage a love of reading that will last a lifetime!

This edition first published in 2009 by Bellwether Media, Inc.

No part of this publication may be reproduced in whole or in part without written permission of the publisher. For information regarding permission, write to Bellwether Media, Inc., Attention: Permissions Department, Post Office Box 19349, Minneapolis, MN 55419.

Library of Congress Cataloging-in-Publication Data
Sexton, Colleen A., 1967–
  Frogfish / by Colleen Sexton.
    p. cm. – (Blastoff! readers. Oceans alive)
  Includes bibliographical references and index.
  Summary: "Simple text and supportive images introduce beginning readers to frogfish. Intended for students in kindergarten through third grade"–Provided by publisher.
  ISBN-13: 978-1-60014-249-9 (hardcover : alk. paper)
  ISBN-10: 1-60014-249-4 (hardcover : alk. paper)
  1. Antennariidae–Juvenile literature. I. Title.

QL638.A577S49 2009
597'.62–dc22   2008033540

Contents

Frogfish live in warm,
shallow waters.

They stay close to the
ocean floor.

5

Frogfish are small, lumpy fish with thick skin.

Most frogfish are about the
size of your hand.

Frogfish bodies can be covered with spots, stripes, and lumps. Some frogfish have sharp **scales**.

Frogfish come in many colors. They can be yellow, red, green, or brown.

Frogfish can slowly change color to match their surroundings.

This **camouflage** helps frogfish look like rocks, plants, or even other animals.

Frogfish have small eyes.
Their mouth looks similar
to a frog's mouth.

gills

Frogfish breathe through **gills**.

Frogfish have a tail and **fins**, but they hardly ever swim.

Instead, frogfish walk across the ocean floor on their bottom fins.

15

Sometimes frogfish want to move fast.

They suck in water. Then they force the water out through their gills and jet forward.

lure

spines

Frogfish have three **spines** on their head. The front spine looks like a rod and a **lure** for fishing.

18

lure

mouth

Frogfish wiggle the lure to draw small fish and other **prey** closer.

Frogfish stay very still.
They spread their mouths wide
open when a fish swims by.

Gulp! Frogfish swallow their prey whole in less than one second!

21

Glossary

camouflage—a covering or coloring that makes an animal look like its surroundings

fins—flaps on a fish's body used for moving, steering, and stopping in the water

gills—organs near the mouth that a fish uses to breathe; the gills move oxygen from the water to the fish's blood.

lure—a body part that hangs from the front spine of a frogfish to draw prey close enough to eat; the frogfish's lure is shaped like a worm, shrimp, or small fish.

prey—an animal that is hunted by another animal for food

scales—small, hard plates that cover the bodies of many fish; some frogfish have scales and others do not.

spine—a hard, sharp part on an animal or plant

To Learn More

AT THE LIBRARY
Lundblad, Kristina and Bobbie Kalman. *Animals Called Fish*. New York: Crabtree, 2005.

Rake, Jody Sullivan. *The Frogfish*. Mankato, Minn.: Capstone, 2008.

Sill, Cathryn P. *About Fish: A Guide for Children*. Atlanta, Ga.: Peachtree, 2002.

ON THE WEB
Learning more about frogfish is as easy as 1, 2, 3.

1. Go to www.factsurfer.com.

2. Enter "frogfish" into the search box.

3. Click the "Surf" button and you will see a list of related Web sites.

With factsurfer.com, finding more information is just a click away.

Index

The images in this book are reproduced through the courtesy of: JUNIORS BILDARCHIV / age fotostock, front cover, p. 15; Getty Images, pp. 4-5; ArteSub / Alamy, p. 6; Hans-Jurgen Mohrmann / age fotostock, p. 7; WaterFrame / Alamy, pp. 8, 16-17; Roger Steene / Image Quest Marine, p. 9; Papilio / Alamy, pp. 10-11; David Fleetham / Alamy, pp. 12-13; Scott Tuason / Image Quest Marine, p. 14; Reinhard Dirscherl, p. 18; RHK UW Productions / Alamy, p. 19; Stephen Frink Collection / Alamy, pp. 20-21.